Discovering
Regional Archaeology:
THE COTSWOLDS AND
THE UPPER THAMES

James Dyer

© James Dyer 1970

Cover: The Whispering Knights legend, Rollright, Oxfordshire—drawn by M. Maitland Howard

SBN 85263107 3

Shire Publications, Tring, Herts.

CONTENTS

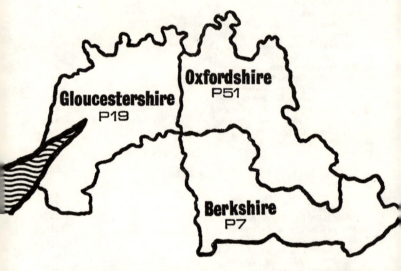

INDEX MAP OF THE COTSWOLDS AND THE UPPER THAMES. The numbers under the county titles refer to the pages on which detailed county maps can be found.

INTRODUCTION

This book is largely concerned with two escarpments, the limestone of the Cotswolds and the chalk of the Berkshire Downs. In both cases the archaeological sites described are linked by prehistoric trackways and trading routes. Although its ancient name is lost, the Jurassic Way runs along the Cotswold edge from Somerset to Lincolnshire; whilst the Berkshire Ridgeway survives as an ancient road for most of the distance between the Thames and Wiltshire. Following the former by car, or the latter on foot, is one of the most delightful ways of spending a few days off the beaten track. Few counties have more to offer by way of ancient monuments than those of the Cotswolds and the Upper Thames.

Many of the sites described in this book are intensively farmed, and visitors are reminded that it is usually necessary to obtain permission before exploring agricultural land. Normally, only the most interesting and easily accessible sites have been described, although one or two earthworks *have* been included that will need a little extra effort on the part of the visitor, where I have felt that they were really worthwhile. The Ordnance Survey 1 inch and 2½ inch maps will be essential in locating most of the sites, and consequently Map numbers and National Grid References have been given throughout. For an explanation of the archaeological terms used, the reader is referred to the key-book in this series *Discovering Archaeology in England and Wales* by James Dyer.

To understand the sites in their true perspective, the material excavated from them should also be studied. Most of this is to be seen in the museums of the region. These are marked with ❁ on the county maps, but are not described in this book. Details of their situation and opening times will be found in the Index Publication *Museums and Galleries in Great Britain and Ireland*.

A number of people have helped with the preparation of this book and have checked some of my entries: to them I extend my gratitude. In particular I must thank E. C. Bowen, FSA, P. M. Greaves, Esq., Jillian Greenaway, Marian and Anthony Hales, Alan McWhirr, FSA, John Real, Esq. and R. A. Rutland, Esq.

Unless otherwise stated, photographs are my own. I am also indebted to Aerofilms Limited, Reading Museum, and the Ministry of Public Building and Works.

1 Alfred's Castle, Ashbury   Iron Age
Map 147   SU : 277822

Approached by bridleway round S. side of Ashdown Park from the B4000. Site lies on N.E. edge of park.

Unusual in that the existing earthwork only encloses about 2 acres, the site lies in fact inside a much larger enclosure, now destroyed, and only visible on aerial photographs. The defence of the 2 acre site consisted of a bank and ditch, with extra external ditch on the south-east, near the original entrance. There may be another entrance at the north-west. The banks were originally faced with sarsen stones, (natural local sandstones) but John Aubrey, writing about 1670, says 'the works are now almost quite spoil'd and defac'd by digging for the Sarsden-Stones (as they call them) to build my Lord Craven's house in the Park'. Large numbers of sarsen stones can still be seen in Ashdown Park.

In spite of this description, the earthworks can be clearly seen today. Pottery of early Iron Age, Romano-British and Saxon date is recorded from the site.

2 Blewburton Hill (Blewbury Camp)   Iron Age
Map 158   SU : 547862

Approached off W. end of bridleroad between Blewbury and Aston Tirrold.

This oval hillfort enclosing 10 acres was excavated by A. E. P. and F. J. Collins between 1947 and 1953, and again in 1967. The first settlement seems to have consisted of a few huts enclosed by a palisade, erected about 350 B.C. and enclosing an area about half the size of the later fort. In the 4th century B.C. the hill was surrounded by a bank held in place by posts on its inner and outer faces, made of material quarried from an external ditch. A gate on the west side was 37 feet wide and may have had an overhead footway. It was given added strength by the presence of a defensive ditch at the back of the entrance, later filled-in.

For some time the fort fell into decay, but around 100 B.C. it was refortified; the ditch was recut and the material thus obtained was dumped on top of the existing bank. The entrance was narrowed to 25 feet and faced with drystone walling. An unusual feature was the presence of horse burials within the entrance area. The end of the occupation of the fort is dated to around A.D. 25 to 50. The excavators thought that this might have been brought about by the advancing

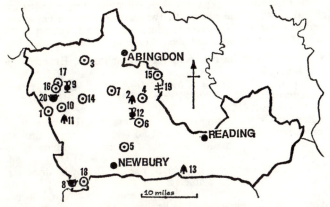

Archaeological sites in Berkshire

Romans, in or around A.D. 43. 'The evident signs of violence, with corpses of animals strewn about the street and covered by the crashed-in ramparts with their retaining walls, plus abundant traces of charcoal perhaps from burnt gateway timbers, could fit such an explanation. But unlike the eastern entrance at Maiden Castle, there is not a shred of evidence to date the disaster. It could equally well have happened as a result of westward Belgic expansion in the years just prior to the Roman conquest.'

During the Anglo Saxon period a cemetery was dug inside the fort. There is nothing to see of this today.

3 Cherbury camp, Kingston Bagpuize   Late Iron Age
Map 158 (Plate 8)   SU : 374963

A mile N. of Charney Bassett by cart track, or S. from A420 passing Race Farm.

This is the only multivallate hillfort in Berkshire. Oval in shape, it has three ramparts separated by ditches, and enclosing 9 acres. Excavation in 1939 showed that the ditches were broad and fairly shallow, the inner rampart faced with dry-stone walling both inside and out, and the other ramparts of dump construction. Leading to the one original entrance on the east side was a metalled roadway with traffic ruts 5 feet apart. The gate had been on the outer side of the entrance passage which had also been lined with drystone walling.

The most unusual thing about this site is its position on low ground. It has been shown that in prehistoric times it

7

formed a narrow-necked peninsula surrounded by marshes on all sides except the north-east (where the entrance causeway ran) thus making it an ideally protected fortress. Pottery from the site is now in the Ashmolean Museum, Oxford.

4 Churn Farm barrow cemetery, Blewbury   Bronze Age
Map 158   SU : 515837
On the S. side of Churn Hill, E. of Churn Farm. Approached by metalled track S.W. from the A417 at Blewbury (SU:527856).

East of Churn Farm are three barrows in a row, measuring respectively 90 feet, 126 feet and 80 feet in diameter and all 3 feet high. A cremation was found in one of the barrows in 1848. ½ mile south-east of the farm (SU : 520833) are two bell-barrows, each about 8 feet high, one is 90 feet in diameter, the other 75 feet in diameter. These have been dug into on a number of occasions. The larger produced a rivetted bronze dagger and a cremation. The line of the Grim's Ditch passes 150 yards south of the barrows. It is not visible. Two other barrows worth looking for in this area are **Churn Knob** (SU:522847) and **Fox Barrow** (SU:506831).

5 Grimsbury Castle, Newbury   Iron Age
Map 158   SU : 512723
In woodland ½ mile S. of Hermitage. A minor road passes through the fort.

This hillfort, situated on sloping ground, is roughly triangular in shape and encloses about 8 acres. It is defended by an inner bank and ditch, with a high outer bank. On the west, some 60 yards from the camp, is a second line of defence. There were three probable entrances, one on the west is slightly incurved with a possible hollow-way leading out of it (as well as a bank of earth some 400 feet long), whilst a third gap in the south-east may have led to springs. Excavations show that the fort was occupied towards the end of the Early Iron Age, producing pottery of Second A and Second B types.

6 Grim's Ditch, Aldworth   Iron Age
Map 158   SU : 546785–570792
One of the best preserved sections of bank and ditch lies east of Beche Farm. ½ mile further east it makes a right-angled turn north. It splits into two where the road from Hungerford Green crosses it. Both forks end after a further ½ mile.

Another section covered with trees lies to the south on Hart Ridge, in Broom Wood and Bowler's Copse (SU:585775). Yet

8

another stretch about ½ mile in length, lies between the A417 near the Grotto (on the Thames) and Hurdle Shaw (SU: 593796). In this area the ditch climbs steeply from the Thames valley, and takes the unusual form of having its ditch facing up the hill-slope. Such a work was almost entirely intended as a boundary and not for defence. At all times the ditch is on the north side of the bank, and its greatest height from ditch bottom to crest of bank is about 6 feet.

7 Grim's Ditch, East and West Hendred to Blewbury
Iron Age

Map 158   SU: 435850–542833
This earthwork lies N. of the Berkshire Ridgeway and can be reached by various field-tracks N. from the Ridgeway. It is best identified by using the Ordnance Survey map.

This earthwork may have been continuous, but it is now broken into a number of sections, largely as a result of agriculture. Its antiquity is demonstrated by the fact that a number of parish boundaries run along it. Its date is uncertain, but current opinion tends to place such earthworks in the Iron Age, often rather as boundaries than defensive works. The greatest height of the earthwork from the crest of the bank to the bottom of the ditch is about 6 feet.

8 Inkpen long barrow (Combe Gibbet)   Neolithic
Map 168   SU: 365623
Beside a bridle path on the ridge between Walbury Hill and Inkpen Hill.

This long barrow is 200 feet long and 75 feet wide, flanked by ditches 15 feet wide and still 3 feet deep. The mound still stands some 6 feet high. Until recently it was crowned by a wooden gibbet.

9 Kingston Lisle Roman barrow   Roman
Map 158   SU: 328882
On E. side of minor road, ½ mile N.N.E. from Kingston Lisle.

The form and position of this barrow suggest that it is of Roman date.

10 Knighton Bushes, Compton Beauchamp
Iron Age/Romano-British

Map 158   Centre at SU: 300830
Approached by minor road from Upper Lambourn, then cart-track.

On the hillside to the west of Knighton Bushes are the

remains of something like 2,000 acres of 'Celtic Fields', together with at least three Romano-British settlements and a cross-dyke. These cover a wide area, stretching almost as far north as the Ridgway, and to Ashdown Park on the west. Little is to be seen of the settlements. One is sub-rectangular in shape and encloses about an acre. It lies due west of Knighton Bushes Plantation at SU: 298831. A second rectangular settlement lies between Woolstone Down and Uffington Down. It is on the north edge of the fields (SU: 302853), but is separated from them by a massive cross-ridge dyke. The third settlement is roughly polygonal in shape and encloses about 2 acres. It lies east of the small wood at Compton Bottom (SU: 286843) and trial excavation produced Romano-British occupation material.

Ancient tracks through the Celtic fields lead from the settlements and join south of the Knighton Bushes Plantation site.

11 Lambourn Seven Barrows and long barrow
Late Neolithic and Bronze Age
Map 158 (Plate 2)   SU: 328828

Mainly situated to the E. of the minor road from Lambourn to Kingston Lyle, 2¼ miles N. of Lambourn.

Although this cemetery contains more than forty burial mounds of probable Bronze Age date, only the group beside the road are accessible and will be described in detail. These barrows lie in two rows running north-west to south-east. I have retained the numbering given them by Mr. Humphrey Case some years ago. Commencing at the north-west end of the row nearest the road, can be seen:

38 A small saucer barrow, 45 feet in diameter, with a ditch 3 feet deep, and slight outer bank.

10 Two barrows enclosed by a single ditch. The mound of one is about 4 feet high, the other 6 feet. A hollow on top of the north mound was made when it was opened by Martin Atkins about 1850. It contained the bones of an ox and a dog.

11 A bowl-barrow, about 10 feet high and 100 feet in diameter. There is no record of its contents although it has certainly been opened.

12 A bowl-barrow with a tree-planting earth ring around it. About 8 feet high and 70 feet in diameter.

13 A fine disc-barrow. 100 feet in diameter, it contains a central mound 60 feet in diameter and 1 foot high. Again, no record exists of its probable opening.

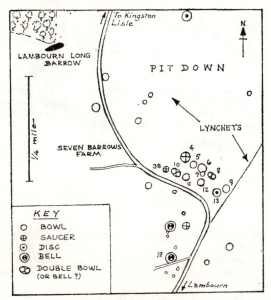

Lambourn Seven Barrows

Second row, furthest from road, north-west end:

4   A large disc or saucer-barrow 120 feet in diameter, with a bank outside the ditch. No record of contents.

5   A bowl-barrow, 70 feet in diameter and 6 feet high. No records.

6 & 7   A large bowl-barrow 80 feet in diameter and 6 feet high, with a tiny barrow on its S. side.

8   Two barrows enclosed within a single ditch, their mounds overlapping suggesting that one is earlier than the other. Both mounds are 6 feet high.

9   A bowl-barrow 60 feet in diameter and 6 feet high. In a sarsen stone cist in this barrow a collared urn was found containing the cremated bones of a woman.

The best bell-barrow at Lambourn is beside the road, some 200 yards south of the group described above. It is partly covered by trees. The mound is 6 feet high and 60 feet wide and is separated from its ditch by a berm 12 feet wide. A cremation burial, together with a bronze awl and a jet pend-

11

ant, were found in a sarsen stone cist, that seems to have been added to the barrow some time after it was built.

A long barrow lies a ¼ mile north at the south end of Wescot Wood (SU: 323834). (Some Ordnance Survey maps show wrong position.) It can be approached along the cart-track which passes over it. It is 270 feet long and 70 feet wide at its east end, where it stands 4 feet high. Excavation showed that it contained a core of sarsen stones, and contained a burial in a rough cist-like setting of sarsen stones, together with some perforated sea-shells.

12 Lowbury Hill, Aston Upthorpe   Roman
Map 158   SU: 540823
2 miles N.E. of Compton along a bridle road.

A rectangular enclosure covers the flint footings of walls. Built in the 4th century A.D., they were perhaps a cattle farm. A pagan Saxon burial was found in the barrow outside the farm entrance.

13 Mortimer Common barrow cemetery   Bronze Age
Map 158   SU: 643651
1½ miles S. of Ufton Nervet on minor road to Stratfield Mortimer which runs over part of the mounds. Situated in a plantation.

There are at least 5 barrows in this group which lie in a straight line north-west to south-east. They consist from the north-west of a disc-barrow, overlaid by a small bell-barrow, then a second bell-barrow 140 feet in diameter and 6 feet high, and finally two small bowl barrows. There is no record of what the barrows contained.

14 Segsbury Camp or Letcombe Castle, Letcombe Regis
                                                 Iron Age
Map 158   SU: 385845
¾ mile W. of A338 along Berkshire Ridgeway. Cart-track passes through centre of camp which is ploughed.

Amongst the larger Berkshire hillforts, Segsbury has an area of 26¼ acres. It has a single bank and ditch defence, with a counterscarp on the north-west side. Like Uffington Castle and Alfred's Castle the bank seems to have been stone faced, sarsen stones having been 'placed in the Banks of the Dike or Trench in form of a Wall', these were 'vast stones, being a red flint, some of which a cart will hardly draw'. Thomas Hearne, who wrote this at the beginning of the 18th century, described cartloads of the stone being removed for local building stone. The main entrance on the east connects the fort to good pasture land and springs. This entrance is flanked by an out-turned rampart. The other breaks in the rampart appear to be modern. In 1871 excavations by Dr. Phené revealed a small stone 'cist' in the rampart on the south side, containing human bones, flint scrapers, a piece of pottery and what seems to have been the *umbo* of a shield. Whilst this sounds like a later Saxon burial, we should not rule out the possibility that this was an Iron Age dedicatory burial, similar to that found at Maiden Castle in Dorset.

15 Sinodun Hills, Castle Hill   Iron Age
Map 158 (Plate 9)   SU : 570924
The road from Sotwell to Little Wittenham climbs up the side of the Sinodun Hills, and a cart track leads to Castle Hill.

This fort is magnificently sited on a steep-sided hill, with wide views in all directions, especially along the Thames valley. Heart-shaped, it encloses about 10 acres, and consists of a deep ditch, the material from which has been thrown down hill to make an outer rampart. There is little trace of an inner bank, although this may well have been buried, by a build-up of plough soil behind it. The entrance on the west is a simple gap. Finds of Iron Age pottery have been made within the camp and outside the entrance. It overlooks the large promontory fort of Dyke Hills (114 acres) which lies on the Dorchester (Oxon) side of the Thames, a mile to the north.

The **Brightwell Barrow** is clearly visible to the east of Castle Hill. It produced Iron Age pottery.

16 Uffington Castle   Iron Age
Map 158   SU : 299864
Approached by car along a one-way road, signposted 'White Horse', from the B4507 near Dragon Hill. There is a car-park at the top. The hillfort lies due E. of this.

A single bank and ditch surround about 8 acres of land. They are broken by an entrance facing north-west. At this point the bank curves outwards along either side of the entrance causeway and seems to join up with a small outer counterscarp bank. Digging by Martin Atkins about 1850 showed that the inner bank seemed to be faced with sarsen stones and also contained two rows of post holes, but it is not clear exactly how they were related to each other.

There are two oval mounds east of the hillfort, above the White Horse, which contained a large number of burials, believed to be Roman when they were opened in the middle of the 19th century. Tradition ascribes many battles to having been fought in this area, and these mounds should perhaps be seriously considered as containing the dead from one of them.

The Berkshire Ridgeway runs along the south side of Uffington Castle. In fine weather it is well worth walking the 1¼ miles west to Wayland's Smithy.

17 Uffington White Horse

Iron Age

Map 158 (Plate 6)   SU: 302866

Best viewed from a distance of 2 or 3 miles to the N., from the Longcot to Fernham road for example (SU:277909). The horse (M.P.B.W.) is approached by car along a signposted one-way road system off the B4507 near Dragon Hill. A ¼ mile walk N.E. from the car-park at the top of the hill leads to the horse, with Uffington Castle on your right.

This curious 'bird-headed' horse, measuring 365 feet from tip of tail to ear, has been carved through the turf into the chalk downland. This probably happened in the late Iron Age, shortly before the birth of Christ, as the design of the horse is very similar to that found on Belgic coins of the period, as well as to the model of a Romano-British horse from Silchester, and modelling on the Iron Age bucket found at Marlborough. It is, perhaps, surprising that the horse has survived for so long. Every few years in the past it had to be cleaned, and many villagers took part in these scourings which were celebrated with festivals which did not die out until the beginning of the present century. Today the Ministry of Public Building and Works are responsible for the upkeep of the figure, and have enclosed it to protect it from damage.

The scouring festivities or 'pastimes' as they came to be called lasted two days, and apart from the actual job of cleaning the horse, involved all the fun of the fair with booths and stalls, races and wrestling, and games and dances of all sorts, usually held inside Uffington Castle earthwork above the horse. Cheeses were raced down the steep hillside in to the dry-valley known as 'The Manger' below.

The reason for cutting the horse is obscure, but most archaeologists consider that it was the tribal emblem of the Dobunni or Atrebates, whose tribe almost certainly occupied the hillfort of Uffington Castle.

There are numerous legends connected with the White Horse. It was, for example, considered lucky to wish when standing on the eye of the horse! The flat-topped hill immediately below the horse is known as Dragon Hill. It was here that tradition says St. George slew the dragon. The bare patch of chalk on the hill is where the dragon's blood spilled on the ground and poisoned the turf. No grass has ever grown there since.

The Blowing Stone referred to in the poem above is a block of natural sarsen stone which stands in the front garden of a cottage (originally the Blowingstone Inn) at the foot of Blowingstone Hill (SU:324871). There is a hole in the stone some 18 inches long, and when it is blown in the correct way, a loud siren-like note is produced which can be heard for two or three miles on a suitable day. There is good reason for thinking that the stone originally stood on White Horse Hill and was removed to its present position about 1750. In spite of a tradition that King Alfred blew through the stone to summon his Saxon warriors, the stone appears to be quite natural and to have no real archaeological significance. Both the Blowing Stone and the White Horse are mentioned by Thomas Hughes in his book *Tom Brown's School Days*. Hughes spent his childhood in the village of Uffington.

18 Walbury hillfort, Combe — Iron Age
Map 168   SU:374617
The minor road from Inkpen to Combe Hill passes beside the fort, and the Berkshire Ridgeway runs through it.

Wallbury hillfort is situated on Combe Hill, the highest chalk hill in Britain, at 974 feet above sea level. Enclosing 82 acres it is the largest hillfort in Berkshire. It is trapezoidal in shape and is surrounded by a single bank and ditch, with faint traces of an outer counterscarp bank. There are two entrances, a small one in the south-east side and a more impressive one, slightly inturned, at the north-west corner. From this corner minor earthworks connected with hollow-ways run north-west down the hill, and in the same area two banks run across the hill spur. The larger west one, a cross-ridge dyke, seems to provide an extra line of defence, whilst the slighter bank, nearer the entrance, may have formed some kind of barbican outwork. It seems likely that circular depressions inside the camp may have been hut circles. The fort is unexcavated.

19 Wallingford Saxon burh — Saxon
Map 158   SU:604893
Clearly seen in park on W. side of town.

The late 9th century document known as the *Burghal Hidage* refers to the fortified town of Wallingford. The earthen defences, originally 3,300 yards in extent, were con-

15

structed by King Alfred or his son Edward at the end of the 9th century. Rectangular in plan, with the Thames forming the eastern side, the defences still survive for some 3,030 yards. They consist of a bank 10 to 12 feet high, with an external ditch of similar depth. The north-east end of the earthwork was destroyed when the later Norman castle was constructed inside the earlier fortification.

20 Wayland's Smithy long barrow, Ashbury   Neolithic
Map 158 (Plate 1)   SU : 281854
½mile S. of Ashbury, and ¼ mile N.E. of the B4000 road, walking along the Berkshire Ridgeway; alternatively 1 mile walking W. from the Uffington Castle car-park.

Beautifully situated in a clump of beech trees, this long-barrow has been proved by excavations in 1962-3 to be of two periods of construction. In Period I a ridge-tent-shaped wooden mortuary chamber had been constructed, with a sarsen stone floor. In this the bodies of some fourteen people had been laid. Whilst some of the bones were articulated, others were quite separate, suggesting that the bodies were stored elsewhere after death for varying lengths of time before being placed in the chamber. When the mortuary building was considered full, sarsen boulders were placed around it, and then chalk from two flanking ditches was piled on top, the whole being retained by a kerb of boulders. All this was covered over in Period II and is not visible today.

The Period II barrow consisted of a trapezoidal mound of chalk 180 feet long and tapering in width from 48 feet to 20 feet. The material for this mound had been quarried from ditches on either side (now filled up) which had been some 6 feet deep and 15 feet wide. The chalk was held in place by a continuous kerb of sarsen stones, which ran over the silted-up ditch of the earlier Period I barrow. At the south end of the new barrow stood six large sarsen slabs, averaging 10 feet high, and flanking the entrance to a stone burial chamber. This chamber is cruciform in plan, and consists of a passage 22 feet long with one stone chamber at either side. The passage was some 6 feet high, and the roof of each chamber 4½ feet high. Gaps between the stone had been filled-in with dry stone walling. Earlier excavations showed that the remains of at least 8 people including a child had come from this barrow. Adjusted Carbon 14 dates suggest that both barrows I and II were constructed between 3,500 B.C. and 3,000 B.C.

Since the barrow was excavated it has been reconstructed, not without some criticism, by the Ministry of Public Building and Works.

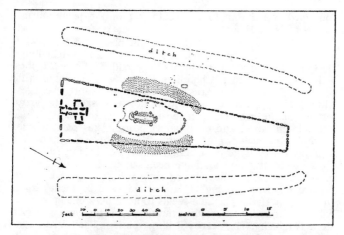

Waylands Smithy (after Atkinson)
Phase I stippled (not visible). Phase II shown in solid line

The legend of Wayland Smith has been told by a number of writers including Sir Walter Scott in *Kenilworth* and Thomas Hughes in *Tom Brown's School Days*. Writing to her father in 1758 the daughter of William Stukeley, the antiquary, wrote:

'. . . the remains of a round temple of the Druids called Wayland Smith. Here the country people have a notion of an invisible smith living there; and if a traveller's horse happens to lose a shoe, leave him there, and a penny, and your horse shall be well shooed.'

The coins, it seems, had to be left on the roofstone of the right-hand burial chamber, known traditionally as the Cave.

GLOUCESTERSHIRE

1 Avening burial chambers
Neolithic
Map 156
ST: 879983
In the village of Avening, at the foot of a steep bank below minor road off A434 and E. of stream.

Three burial chambers were moved to this site in 1806 after the excavation of a long barrow in which they were

17

contained, which lay to the south-east of the neighbouring hamlet of Nags Head.

The chambers are all rectangular in plan, and from west to east measure respectively, I, 3 feet wide and 5 feet long; II, 3 feet wide and 5 feet 8 inches long; and III, 6 feet 7 inches wide and 6 feet long. Chambers II and III are roofed with single capstones and are approached by short passages. Chamber I has neither a capstone nor a passage. The great interest in the group lies in the fact that chamber III has a porthole entrance, and chamber II possibly has part of one. Porthole entrances consist of artificially-cut holes large enough to allow the passage of a human body. At Avening chamber III semi-circular notches have been cut in the upright edges of two adjoining stones closing the entrance, and these have formed an oval opening 16 inches wide and 33 inches high. In chamber II the porthole seems to have been cut in a stone lying horizontally across the entrance, a corresponding upper stone is missing. The nearby Rodmarton long barrow also had portholes (no longer visible: see page 46) and such features, although rare, are found elsewhere in Britain and western Europe.

2 Bagendon

Iron Age

Map 157   SP: 018064

Off the A435, ½ mile E. of the modern village of Bagendon.

This area of about 200 acres, defended on three sides by earthworks, and on the fourth by forest, may possibly have been the *oppidum* or tribal headquarters of the Belgic people known as the Dobunni. Coin moulds and many coins suggest that the Dobunni had their mint at Bagendon around 20–30 A.D. Italian red pottery and bronze and iron brooches made by continental craftsmen, indicate that the *oppidum* was flourishing at this time. Excavations have suggested that the site was occupied from about A.D. 15 to A.D. 60.

The main dykes run for 600 yards beside Welsh Way near Perrot's Brook and for ¼ mile along the west side of Cutham Lane. A second line of ditches lies 250 feet east of this latter site. When the earthwork beside Cutham Lane was excavated the ditch was shown to be 10 feet 6 inches wide and 6 feet deep. About a mile north of the main system runs the earthwork called **Scrubditch** (SP:010077). Although its ditch faces south and therefore seems to oppose the Bagendon earthworks, it is generally interpreted as part of their system.

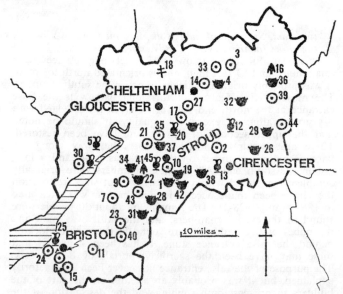

Archaeological sites in Gloucestershire

3 Beckbury Camp, Hailes Abbey   Iron Age
Map 144   SP : 064299
*On the summit of a hill ½ mile E. of Hailes Abbey. Can
be approached by tracks through Hailes Wood from Hailes
to Farmcote minor road.*

This is a small rectangular promontory fort enclosing about
4½ acres. Its north and west sides are defended by steeply
falling ground. A single upstanding rampart and silted ditch
bound the east and south sides. Although there may have been
entrances around the rampart ends at the north-east and
south-west corners, the real access seems to have been by a
hollow-way at the north-west undefended corner. A length of
drystone outer facing wall is exposed at the north end of the
east rampart.

There are fine views from this little fort, particularly to the
south-west where the opposite valley slopes show considerable
disturbance, perhaps connected with a deserted medieval
village.

4 Belas Knap long barrow, Charlton Abbots   Neolithic
Map 144   SP : 021254
*Signposted footpath leaves minor road from Winchcombe
to Charlton Abbots at SP:022261. Small lay-by for one or*

two cars. Steep climb and walk of ½ mile, but well-worth the effort for the view. M.P.B.W. open at any time.

This beautiful long barrow is 170 feet long, 60 feet wide (maximum) and 13 feet high, and is orientated north to south. It was probably originally higher to cover the south chamber. The most striking feature of this long barrow is the false entrance at the north end, between convex horns edged with dry-stone walling of exceptional quality. It should be noted that the upper sections of this walling have been restored. There are a pair of burial chambers half-way along the barrow, a third chamber on the south-east side, and a long cist in the south end. All of these chambers were originally completely enclosed within the barrow, but since restoration they have been made accessible. The barrow was excavated in 1863-5 and 1928-31. The remains of about 30 people were found in the burial chambers, and the skull of a man and the bones of five children were found in the rubble blocking behind the false entrance stone. It has been suggested that these may have been the sacrificial burials of Beaker folk. The purpose of the false entrance has never been satisfactorily explained, but it was probably an attempt on the part of the builders to prevent tomb robbing and the desecration of the graves of their ancestors. The name Belas Knap is medieval in origin and means a beacon mound.

A small ploughed-out round barrow can be seen as a low mound in the ploughed field due west of the long barrow.

5 Blackpool Bridge Roman road, Forest of Dean   Roman
Map 156 (Plate 13)   SO: 653087
Minor road N. off B4431, beyond former railway bridge.

A fine stretch of paved Roman road with curb edging and marks of wheeled traffic. It was part of the industrial road from Ariconium (SO: 645235) which connected the Forest of Dean iron workings with the main road system along the south coast of Wales.

6 Blaise Castle hillfort, Bristol   Iron Age
Map 156   ST: 559784
On the Blaise Castle estate, S.W. of Folk Museum.

This oval hillfort of about 6 acres, commands a wide view of the Severn estuary. Steep sides on the south and south-east made only a slight defence necessary, but along the north and west there are two banks and ditches. Except for the highest point, the site is largely wooded, but access is eased by the footpaths laid out at the beginning of the 19th century. The original entrances are unknown at present, but excavation may reveal them, as it has recently produced Iron Age 'B' pottery, jewellery and storage pits.

7 Bloody Acre Camp, Cromhall
Iron Age

Map 156   ST: 689915

Wooded. In Tortworth Park (H.M. Prison) beside minor road ½ mile N. of Cromhall.

This is probably the best of a small group of hillforts between the Cotswolds and the Severn. It is basically a promontory fort with steep sides overlooking a small stream 100 feet below. The promontory is cut-off on the west side by banks and ditches which isolate some 10 acres. On the south-west these earthworks consist of 3 large banks with silted ditches between them. Only two of the banks survive at the north end of the defences, at which point the inner bank turns east perhaps forming part of an uncertain inturned entrance.

8 West Tump long barrow, Birdlip
Neolithic

Map 143   SO: 912133

In Buckle Wood W. of B4070.

This long barrow is 150 feet long and 76 feet wide. It is contained within dry-stone walls and has a visible false-entrance at the east end. When opened in 1880 a single chamber 15 feet long and 4 feet wide was found at the end of a passage 7 feet long, leading in from the south side. It contained some 20 disordered burials, together with one at the back of the chamber which was raised on five stones. This was the skeleton of a young woman, with the remains of a baby nearby. Four more skeletons were found lying in the forecourt near the false entrance.

9 Brackenbury Ditches, North Nibley
Iron Age

Map 156   ST: 747949

Wooded site beside B4060. Can be approached by turning off minor road N.W. of Bournstream.

A promontory fort of about 6 acres sited on a west facing spur of the Cotswolds. A bank and ditch follow the contour of the steep hillside; whilst two banks and ditches mark the north-east side, these are widely spaced in the south-western manner. What appears to be the original entrance is approached by a hollow-way in the south side. A number of pits in the vicinity are probably of natural origin.

10 The Bulwarks, Minchinhampton   Iron Age

Map 156 (Plate 12)   SO: 857004 to SO: 869012

Scattered over Minchinhampton Common (National Trust Property). Use sketch-map for identification, and beware of wandering golfers.

Of all Cotswold earthworks few are more tantalising than the maze of banks and ditches that are scattered over Minchinhampton Common, and few have provoked such a variety of interpretations.

The earthworks seem to fall into two main groups depending on the boldness of their architecture. By far the most impressive and probably the oldest earthwork in Group I is the 1½ mile long dyke known as the Bulwarks (No. 1 on plan), which is curved to face the south-east, and isolates an area to the north-west of at least 600 acres. Excavation of the Bulwarks about 1937 revealed that the ditch had been cut into the solid rock, it was 23 feet wide at ground level, reducing to 5 feet wide at the bottom and 8 feet deep. The material from it had been used to construct the bank which is 30 feet wide today and 5 feet high. A vertical drystone wall was used to retain the bank and prevent it from falling into the ditch.

The problem presented by the Bulwarks is the direction in which it is facing. If it is protecting land to the north-west then we may have to consider it as part of a large Iron Age complex perhaps connected with an agricultural economy requiring cattle and sheep penning areas, and cutting off a 2 miles long ridge stretching north-west to Rodborough. Bearing in mind the size of the Stanwick earthworks in Yorkshire, this is not out of the question. Alternatively it has been suggested that the Bulwarks originally surrounded the area now occupied by the village of Minchinhampton; this means accepting an inner ditch and a much smaller enclosed area of some 200 acres.

The only other Group I earthwork is a length of rampart and south-east facing ditch 200 yards west of the reservoir (No. 2 on plan). This cross-ridge dyke stops suddenly and without obvious cause in the middle of the plateau. It is 260 yards long, and excavation in 1937 showed that its ditch was 23 feet wide at the top, 11 feet wide at the bottom and 8 feet deep. Behind it, to the north-west was a bank of limestone rubble 32 feet wide and 4 feet high. Like the Bulwarks it produced Iron Age pottery, and the two earthworks are probably contemporary.

Earthworks of the 2nd Group are lesser affairs with distinct banks averaging some 2 feet high and 5 feet wide, and ditches

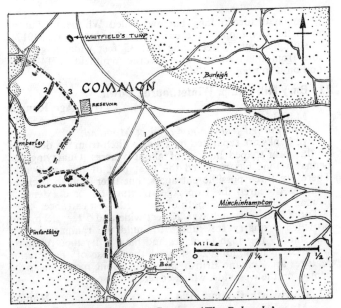

Minchinhampton Common 'The Bulwarks'

of similar depth and 4 to 5 feet wide. They form two arcs on the west side of the Common. Earthwork No. 3 on the plan has sometimes been referred to as 'Amberley Camp'. No. 4 almost joins it to the south. Both these earthworks are too slight to be of any great antiquity and are probably connected with field boundaries of fairly recent times. Both of these banks cut across a number of minor earthworks, which tend to be low, slight banks almost invisible except to the trained eye, and presumably earlier in date than No. 3 and 4. They may indeed be connected with the cattle pens referred to above.

Before leaving the Common we should also notice some of the 40 or more curious rectangular mounds known as pillow mounds. Averaging 50 feet in length, 10 feet wide and 2 feet high they are scattered all over the plateau and seem to be fairly recent in date. Opinions differ as to their use; it is usually suggested that they were artificial rabbit warrens. A good example can be easily found at the west end of the cattle trough that lies midway between the reservoir and the Golf House.

23

A much disturbed long barrow, called Whitfield's Tump, lies on the Common to the east of Littleworth (SO:854017). Measuring about 75 feet long and 35 feet wide, it gets its name from the tradition that George Whitfield (1714-1770) stood on it to preach in 1743.

11 Bury Hill Camp, Winterbourne Down

Iron Age/Roman

Map 156   ST:652791

Approached from minor road at Moorend.

Two banks are separated by a single ditch from the defences of this pear-shaped hillfort of about 5 acres. Quarrying for pennant stone has removed the west part of the earthwork. There are three possible entrances, but later Roman occupation has obscured the Iron Age structure to some extent. A Roman well was found south of the north-west entrance.

The 'U' shaped ditch was 20 feet wide and 5 feet deep, and provided a quarry for rubble to build the ramparts which still stand 9 feet high in places and have a drystone retaining wall. Excavation in 1926 showed that most of the interior features are Romano-British, including a long mound near the centre, on the west side, which covers a house.

12 Chedworth Roman villa

Roman

Map 144   SP:053134

A National Trust property off the A429 at Fossebridge, signposted along Yanworth to Withington road. (Not road to Chedworth village.) Open 10.00 to 13.00 hours, 14.00 to 19.00 hours (or dusk if earlier). Closed on Mondays (except Bank Holidays) first 15 days of October and throughout January. Car-park beside villa.

This is the finest of more than a dozen Roman villas found within ten miles of Cirencester. It was accidentally discovered in 1864 whilst digging for a lost ferret, and has since been extensively excavated. The site chosen was beside a spring in a small wooded valley with wide views to the east. The villa began life as a number of separate buildings along the sides and end of the valley in the first half of the 2nd century A.D. The original house stood at the head of the valley; it was smaller than at present and lacked the bath suite, which at that time stood apart, at the west end of what was to become the north wing. A small half-timbered building stood on the site of the south wing. This, together with the main house, was destroyed by fire and later restored, early in the 3rd century. At the same time the north wing was extended, and the bath-house enlarged. It was early in the 4th century that all the buildings were drawn together by the construction of a continuous corridor, which created an inner courtyard which would have contained a formal garden. On the south side of this court lay the kitchen and latrines, and a steward's room that jutted out into the courtyard. Beyond the kitchen was a furnace room which heated a large new dining room with mosaic pavements depicting the four seasons. This was situated at the south end of the west wing. At the north end a new set of Turkish baths were constructed. The old baths were reconstructed as a suite of Swedish or Spartan baths, which were equipped with large cold plunges (for many years these were mistaken for a fullery).

Beyond the north-west corner of the villa lies the spring which supplied water to the site. This was covered by a small apsidal building, the Nymphaeum. Inside was an octagonal basin which continually held fifteen hundred gallons of water, and still continues to supply the present house on the site. Other reservoirs would almost certainly have been needed to supplement the supply to such a large house. Originally dedicated to a water goddess, the spring later became a Christian shrine as is witnessed by the *Chi-Rho* symbols carved on its stone surround. A further dining room and guest suite with hypocaust was added late in the 4th century, in the north wing, east of the Swedish baths. Nothing remains of the east end of the south wing. Life in the villa seems to have come to an end late in the 4th century.

The original approach to the villa was from the White Way, through the wood to the north-east. This track passed close to a barrow which produced the cremation urn, now in the site museum. Close to the river Colne $\frac{1}{2}$ mile south-east of the villa stood a square pagan temple which produced the hunting relief, also exhibited in the museum.

The museum was built by Lord Eldon on the east side of the Inner Court in 1866. It contains, in rather cramped conditions, most of the objects found on the site and a reconstruction model of the villa itself.

13 Cirencester (Corinium Dobunnorum) Roman town
Map 157   SP : 0202

The Corinium Museum makes a useful starting point, since there is not a great deal to see of the Roman town. Situated in Park Street, the Museum is open on weekdays from 10 a.m. to 1 p.m., 2 p.m. to 5.30 p.m. from July to September; 10 a.m. to 1 p.m., 2 p.m. to 4.30 p.m. from October to June, inc. Saturdays. Sundays 2 to 4.30 p.m. June to August. The local archaeological society also has a small museum next door to the Corinium Museum which is well worth a visit.

Cirencester began as a civilian settlement outside a small fort. The position was a good one at the junction of five important roads and a river crossing. However the siting of the earliest fort on marshy ground at Watermoor was at fault, and it was soon moved 500 yards north to an area bounded by the Avenue, Chester Street, Watermoor Road and St. Michael's Fields.

Not long after A.D. 60 a gradual movement of native tribesmen began from the Dobunnic centre, perhaps at Bagendon three miles to the north into the more attractive Romanised settlement. By about A.D. 75 the fort was dismantled, and all trace of it was buried beneath the expanding township which became the tribal administrative centre for the Dobunni, *Corinium Dobunnorum.* A grid of streets was laid out, the position of which is still followed by Lewis Lane and Watermoor Road. A forum and basilica were constructed, as well as many shops and private houses. The position of the walls forming the apse of the **basilica** are marked in a cul-de-sac which opens off the south-east side of the Avenue opposite Tower Street.

As the town developed during the 2nd century, an **amphitheatre** was constructed, at first of timber and earth, but later rebuilt in stone. It survives today and is known as The Bullring. Its grass-covered banks still stand 27 feet high, and excavation has shown that they were originally terraced with low limestone walls which probably supported wooden seats. Two opposing entrance passages are still visible, that on the north being 96 feet long and lined with stone walls. The major axis of the arena measures 160 feet, the minor axis 134 feet 6 inches. The amphitheatre can be reached by a footpath 250 yards west of the railway bridge in Cotswold Avenue.

Earthen defences with two external ditches and masonry towers were constructed during the second half of the 2nd century; thus enclosing some 240 acres. At the same time at least one gate (the Verulamium Gate) with twin semi-circular towers and an adjoining bridge over the river Churn were set-up on the road to St. Albans and Leicester. About A.D. 220 the defences were strengthened by cutting back the earthen rampart and inserting a stone wall 10 feet thick; and later, in the 4th century external stone bastions were added. Parts of the earthen rampart and wall can now be seen north-west of the London Road and in the Abbey Gardens, whilst a good section exists in the Beeches, Watermoor Gardens, south-east of London Road.

A number of changes occurred to the forum and basilica early in the 4th century, which may perhaps be explained by the raising of the status of the town to a provincial capital. It is likely that life continued at *Corinium* until well into the 5th century and beyond. Indeed it is likely that part of the town survived at the time of the battle of Dyrham in A.D. 577 when four British kings were defeated and Cirencester fell into Saxon hands.

14 Cleeve Hill promontory fort, Cheltenham   Iron Age
Map 144   SO:985255
Lay-by on A46 3½ miles N.E. of Cheltenham at SO:985269. Long uphill walk across Cleeve Hill Common (magnificent views). Alternative route along minor road from same point on A46 to Nutterswood. Very steep climb up to fort.

This small 2 acre promontory fort is isolated by two semi-circular ramparts, each with external ditches. A berm separates the inner ditch from the outer rampart. No entrance exists, and we may assume that access was originally gained around the ends of the ramparts, now quarried or eroded away. A golf green has destroyed part of the outer rampart and ditch on the north side, and visitors should keep a wary eye open for golfers who constantly bombard the fort with golf balls.

About a third of a mile north of the fort is a linear earthwork running east to west just south of the trigonometrical station on the highest point of the hill. It has a ditch on its south (fort facing) side.

Also on the hill, not far from the A46 road, is an earthwork known as The Ring. This is a circular banked and ditched enclosure about 100 feet in diameter, that has been utilised to contain a disused golf green. It is almost certainly of ancient construction.

15 Clifton Down Camp, Bristol   Iron Age
Map 156   ST:566733
North of the Clifton suspension bridge. Observatory stands inside the fort.

This is one of three forts defending promontories and facing one another across the Avon Gorge. The other two, Borough Walls and Stokeleigh, are in Somerset. All are less than a quarter of a mile from each other. They are also similar in construction and may be contemporary, but the steep cliffs of the Avon Gorge and the river 250 feet below, make access between the forts difficult, although a ford is known to have existed across the river, a few yards below the suspension bridge, until at least 120 years ago.

The multivallate ramparts of Clifton Down Camp enclose some 3 acres, and form an arc, which is broken by a probable entrance on the east side. There may have been a further entrance close to the edge of the cliff on the north-west. The ramparts have been disturbed by quarrying and are obscured by bushes, but paths follow the lines of the ditches. On the south-west side of the interior is a bank and a rectangular earthwork which has not been excavated, and is regarded by most authorities as being of later workmanship.

16 Cow Common barrow cemetery, Swell

Neolithic/Bronze Age

Map 144   SP: 132263

2½ miles W. of Lower Swell, on N. of minor road from Swell Hill Farm to Chalk Hill. Footpath N.E. leaves corner of wood to cross Cow Common.

Within a distance of 400 yards lies a cemetery of ten round barrows and one long barrow. The long barrow is of the false entrance type and is 150 feet long and 5 feet high. Two stone chambers contained ten adult burials and one infant, as well as neolithic pottery and pieces of pottery spoons.

The round barrows vary in size and height from 30 to 60 feet in diameter and 1 to 4 feet high. Amongst five in an overlapping row at the west end of the Common, one contained a crouched male burial in a stone cist, with two later cremated burials in urns (one with a bronze razor) added to the barrow at a later Bronze Age date. Another contained a beehive-shaped chamber similar to that at Bibury (see Lamborough Banks, page 32), and the other three all contained cremations. Nothing is known of the contents of the remaining barrows that lie west, south-west, and east of the long barrow.

17 Crickley Hill, Coberley

Iron Age

Map 144   SO: 928161

Extreme W. end of National Trust property opposite Air Balloon public house. Can be approached off A417 W. of roundabout, along minor road signposted 'Cold Slad ¼ mile', and climbing steep hillside.

This is a simple promontory fort in which an area of about 9 acres is defended by a main rampart some 9 feet high at its east end, with an external ditch, proved by excavation to be

8 feet deep. Some 200 yards further west is a second lesser rampart. The sides of the promontory are steep and rugged and have been exaggerated by modern quarrying, traces of which can be found all over the hill. (A low mound lying in a hollow at the west end of the hill may cover traces of a quarry railway.) There is an entrance passage curving into the north end of the main rampart, which has been slightly destroyed by quarry work. Recent excavations by Philip Dixon suggest a number of periods of occupation on the hill, including at least two builds of the main rampart, both incorporating drystone walls; the first, with lacing timbers, was destroyed by burning.

On the west of the A417 road in Emma's Grove wood, south of the A436 junction and roundabout, are three **round barrows,** one large and two small. Nothing is known of their contents and it has been suggested that the larger may have been a castle mound (SO: 935159).

18 Deerhurst Church   Saxon
Map 143   SO: 871299
Approached by minor road off B4213, the church lies on N. side of village.

Parts of this Anglo-Saxon church belonged to a monastery existing in A.D. 804. These included the original nave, lower part of the west porch and the east side chapels. The architectural history of the church is complicated, but Mr. E. C. Gilbert has outlined four initial phases of development.

1) Nave (60 feet long) and chancel.
2) West porch (two storeys high) and north and south side chapels, (each of two storeys).
3) West porch raised to three storeys with double triangular-headed east window looking into the nave. Window and door arches surviving from this period have heads with either flat lintels, or triangles made-up of two inclined stones.
4) In the 10th century arched doorways were introduced, the west porch was raised again to become a tower, the apsidal chancel was probably rebuilt.

The church contains seventeen doorways and fourteen windows of Anglo-Saxon construction, and a late 9th century font, together with items of Saxon sculpture including a Madonna in the west porch and an angel panel in the apse.

200 yards south-west of the church stands Odda's chapel, also of Anglo-Saxon date, and until 1885 thought to be an ordinary half-timbered farmhouse.

19 Gatcombe Lodge chambered long barrow   Neolithic
Map 156   ST: 884997
On the S. side of the minor road from Minchinhampton
to Avening, in the trees at the N. end of Gatcombe Park.
This long barrow has a false entrance at its north-east end
between drystone horns. The barrow measures 180 feet by
70 feet and is orientated north-east to south-west. There is an
accessible burial chamber on the north side of the barrow
not far from the east end. It contained a single skeleton when
it was discovered in 1871. The chamber is constructed of five
upright stones with a capstone, and some fine drystone walling. Two more stones form an entrance. Near the south-west
end is a large slab of stone which may be the coverstone to
another chamber.
Some 300 yards north of the long barrow stands **The Long
Stone** (ST:884999). This upright triangular slab of oolite stands
7½ feet high, and may be part of a burial chamber destroyed
in the 19th century. Holes in the stone appear to be natural.
A smaller stone block is built into a wall 12 yards away.

20 Great Witcombe villa   Roman
Map 143   SO: 899142
Ministry of Works signpost on A417 ¼ mile E. of cross-
road with A46. 1½ miles S. of road along rough track past
Droy's Court. Cars may be parked in farmyard. Key at
the farm.
This beautifully sited villa lies at the foot of the Cotswolds
close to springs. It has been excavated on three occasions to
reveal rooms on three sides of a courtyard, including a bath
suite with hypocausts and mosaic pavements; the latter with
geometric and aquatic designs. The walls of the rooms were
brightly painted in colours which we, today, would probably
consider garish. Small pots containing some of the paint were
found during the excavations. The visible remains date from
the middle of the 3rd century to the end of the 4th. The
villa is in the care of the Ministry of Public Building and
Works.

21 Haresfield Beacon (Ring Hill), Haresfield
Iron Age/Roman
Map 156   SO: 823090
Minor road from Haresfield to Whiteshill passes through
the earthwork. National Trust property.
Haresfield Beacon and Ring Hill were initially enclosed

within a single rampart and ditch forming a fort of some 16 acres. There seems to have been an oblique entrance on the south side of Ring Hill. Later the earthworks were doubled in area by adding an extension east to enclose Haresfield Hill. A notable feature of the site are the wide views it commands of the Severn valley.

22 Hetty Peggler's Tump long barrow, Uley   Neolithic
Map 156 (Plate 3)   SO: 789000
Signposted from the B4066. Key from house ½ mile S. beside main road. Electric torch or candle required.

This long barrow measures 120 feet by 85 feet, and lies east to west on a high ridge at the edge of the Cotswolds overlooking the vales of Berkeley and Severn. The burial chamber lies at the east end beyond a deep forecourt. It belongs to the type of stone-built chamber known as a 'transepted gallery grave' which means that it consists of a passage 22 feet long with two chambers on either side, rather like the transepts of a church. (The two on the right (north) have been sealed off in modern times.) There is also a chamber at the end of the passage. The walls and roof are composed of large slabs of stone filled in with areas of drystone-work. Excavations in 1821 revealed 15 skeletons, and 8 or 9 others were found in 1854.

The name derives from Hester Peggler who was the owner, or owner's wife, in the 17th century.

23 Horton Camp hillfort, Chipping Sodbury   Iron Age
Map 156   ST: 765845
Accessible from minor roads ¼ mile S. of Horton village.

This rectangular promontory fort of 5 acres crowns a steep-sided hill. Its defences consist of a single bank and ditch which are best preserved under fir trees on the north-east side, although the ditch is largely silted up. The site has been too much damaged to reveal its original entrance. Its position less than a mile north of Sodbury Camp may be significant, since both lie on the same ridge looking west across the upper Frome valley. The camp is normally under grass.

24 King's Weston Hill, Bristol   Iron Age
Map 156   ST: 557782
Minor road or footpath from B4057.

This small fort lies ¼ mile south-west of Blaise Castle hillfort, at the north-east end of a narrow hill ridge. A single bank and ditch cut across the hillspur 300 yards west of the camp. Between this bank and the main fort is a small roughly circular banked and ditched enclosure, about 60 yards in diameter. Excavation in 1956 has shown it to be contemporary with the main fort. The ditch of the latter was cut into solid rock, and was 6 feet deep and 15 feet wide, with a flat floor and vertical sides. Philip Rahtz, the excavator, was of the opinion that the owners of the fort might have been driven out, by slingstones from the neighbouring Blaise Castle hill-fort.

25 King's Weston villa, Bristol (Sea Mills villa)   Roman
Map 156   ST: 534776
At the side of the Portway, at its junction with Roman Way. On N. side of King's Weston Hill, close to W. end of Long Cross. Guide book available.

Excavated in 1948-50, accessible, with a wooden shed over part of the site. Built late in the 3rd century this villa was altered a number of times before it was abandoned towards the end of the 4th century. Basically the house consists of east and west wings, linked by a corridor and porch. The back wall of the corridor was arched and looked out onto a gravelled court, around which other rooms were ranged. Unfortunately these latter could not be excavated. Beside the west wing were five rooms forming a bath suite. Only three rooms are now visible. Room 6 houses a site museum and contains a floor mosaic from a Roman villa at Brislington (Bristol). Room 7 contains a poor geometric mosaic laid between A.D. 270 and 300. There are two other mosaics of the same period in the house.

The villa was one of a number in the Roman port of *Abona* (Sea Mills) which grew up at the point where the river Trym flowed into the Avon.

26 Lamborough Banks chambered long barrow, Bibury
                                                      Neolithic
Map 157   SP: 107094
Approached on minor road from N. of Salt Way. Situated in Lamborough Banks covert.

Orientated north-west to south-east this badly damaged long barrow is 280 feet long and 100 feet wide at its broadest end. It is surrounded by a double dry-stone wall, each facing out-wards, with rubble between them. Early excavations showed that at the south end the walls curve slightly inwards to a false entrance stone. A stone chamber (consisting of four wall slabs at each side and one at each end) was found in the narrow (north-west) end of the barrow in 1854. It contained a single burial.

1. The facade of the Period II long barrow of Wayland's Smithy, Berkshire, reconstructed after its excavation in 1962. (Ministry of Public Building and Works.)

2. The inhumation burial found in the head of the mound of the Lambourn long barrow, Berkshire (Reading Museum and Art Gallery.)

3. *The entrance to Hetty Peggler's Tump (the Uley barrow) Gloucestershire, lies beyond a deep forecourt.*

4. *The Whispering Knights, Oxon., consist of four upright stones and a fallen capstone, that were once part of a burial chamber.*

5. *The King's Men: an aerial view of the Rollright Stones which, according to tradition, are uncountable. (Aerofilms Ltd.)*

6. *The White Horse carved on the chalk downs at Uffington was probably an Iron Age tribal symbol. It resembles horses depicted in art of the period. (Ashmolean Museum.)*

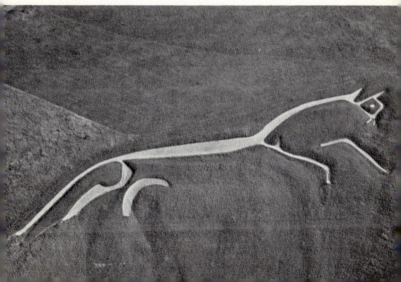

7. The stone walls of Chastleton Burrow hill-camp, now covered with trees, enclose 3½ acres. The fort is unusual in having no quarry ditch. (Aerofilms Ltd.)

8. Cherbury Camp in Berkshire is sited on low-lying ground and probably relied on marshland for added protection. (Aerofilms Ltd.)

9. Castle Hill hillfort is magnificently sited on the Sinodun Hills in Berkshire, above the Thames valley. (*Aerofilms Ltd.*)

10. Sodbury Camp is one of the finest multivallate hillforts in the Cotswolds. The widely-spaced ramparts are a peculiarity of the area. (*Aerofilms Ltd.*)

11. The Dyke Hills at Dorchester-on-Thames isolate a promontory fort of 114 acres. They appear as a double line across the centre of the picture. Beyond are the Sinodun Hills and in the foreground the site of the Roman town of Dorchester, Oxon. (*Aerofilms Ltd.*)

12. The Bulwarks Iron Age dyke stretches for $1\frac{1}{2}$ miles across Minchinhampton Common, Gloucestershire. Excavation has shown that the ditch is 8 feet deep.

13. *The paved Roman road at Blackpool Bridge in the Forest of Dean, Gloucestershire. Notice the use of curbstones. (David Uttley.)*

14. Excavations in 1928 at Lydney revealed a Roman guest-house, bath suite, iron mines and the temple, now overgrown, shown in the picture.

15. This Anglo-Saxon carving of the crucifixion is on the outside of the porch of St. Matthew's church, Langford, Oxon.

A short distance south-east of Lamborough Banks in an adjoining copse is a long, low, irregular mound some 150 feet in length, with a beehive-shaped chamber in its south side. The chamber is about 5½ feet in diameter and has walls 4 feet thick. There is a low bench all round the cell and three cupboard-like niches in the walls. The upper part of the domed roof is missing. This cell resembles other corbelled chambers in Gloucestershire at Bibury and Cow Common, and is probably of neolithic construction. There is no evidence to show that they were used for burials.

27 Leckhampton Hill hillfort and barrow   Iron Age
Map 144   SO: 948184
Approached from S. by minor road to Hartley Farm off B4070. Car park at SO:951178 and ½ mile walk (signposted 'Devil's Chimney') to fort.

This is a semi-circular promontory fort, enclosing about 8 acres. It is surrounded by a single rampart about 6 feet high, with an external rock-cut ditch. The rampart was dry-stone faced and showed considerable signs of burning on the east side when examined. The entrance is also on the east (200 feet north of the point where the modern road enters) and excavations in 1969-70 have clarified earlier reports (1925) of stone guard chambers which have been shown to lie on either side of the entrance passage. The steep cliff-like north and west sides are the results of modern quarrying, but the fort would almost certainly have relied on very steep natural slopes for defence on these sides.

Outside the fort and north of the point where the road enters, is what appears to be a round barrow enclosed by a square bank and ditch. It is very overgrown and its form is difficult to see. Limited excavation failed to reveal a burial. It may have been the site of a Celtic shrine.

28 Leighterton long barrow, 'West Barrow'   Neolithic
Map 156   ST: 819913
W. of Leighterton village, on road to Boxwell. Covered with trees and enclosed within modern stone wall.

One of the largest chambered long barrows in the Cotswolds, it lies east to west, and is about 270 feet long and 20 feet high. Three arched burial chambers were excavated in 1703, but they are no longer visible. John Aubrey referred to a stone standing 'at the great end' of the barrow, but this, too, has vanished. It is probable that this was a false-entrance grave, like Belas Knap.

29 Lodge Park long barrow, Eastington

Neolithic

Map 144

SP: 142125

In Lodge Park, 2 miles S.E. of Northleach.

This chambered long barrow is 150 feet long, 75 feet wide and 8 feet high. Two upright stones and the cover stone of the entrance can be seen at the wider south-east end. The whole mound is orientated south-east to north-west.

30 Lydney hillfort, temple, etc.

Iron Age, Roman, etc.

Map 156 (Plate 14)

SO: 616027

Situated in Lydney Park. This is a private deer park and permission to visit must be sought in writing from the agent at Lydney Park Estate Office. Access from the A48(T) at SO:623021 and through farm.

A steep-sided promontory fort, enclosing some 5 acres, was constructed during the 1st century B.C., by erecting two banks with external ditches across the north-east end of the spur. There were two probable entrances one at the south tip of the spur had inturned flanks, and a second lay at the south limit of the earthworks on the east side. The gap in the north rampart is of recent origin. The rampart was composed of rubble with an outer kerb of large stones; it supported a roughly paved rampart walk some 5 feet wide. It seems likely that the inner bank on the east side is a later, but pre-Roman, addition to the defences.

The inhabitants seem to have spent uninterrupted lives till well into the 4th century A.D., living in rectangular timber huts and making deep, rounded pots of a type common in the Bristol Channel area, known, somewhat unfortunately, as 'flower pots'. They produced metal work, including brooches, and mined iron on the site. Two iron mines have now been found and one is visible, its entrance marked by a trap-door, some 40 yards along the east side of the plateau, north of the Adam and Eve statues. It extends 50 feet underground and reaches a depth of 15 feet. It cuts through the Iron Age rampart, which was later rebuilt over the gallery. The mine was being worked not later than the 3rd century. Original pick-marks can still be seen on the ferruginous walls of the mine. (Prospective visitors are warned to take protective clothing and torches.) The second mine lies under the Roman bath suite on the west side of the site.

Towards the end of the 3rd century A.D. the prehistoric rampart was given a minor rebuild. Shortly after A.D. 364 a large temple with a guest house and bath suite were erected in the south half of the hillfort. The temple, which measures

80 feet by 60 feet, was entered by a flight of steps from the south-east. These led into a 10 feet wide corridor which passed round the four sides of a rectangular *cella* or sanctuary. This *cella* was divided into three smaller sanctuaries. Outside in the corridor were seven alcoves or 'chapels' which are a unique feature, each with a mosaic pavement in front of them. The temple was dedicated to the native British cult of Nodens (Nodons) who was concerned with healing, the sun and water. His concern for healing clearly attracted many visitors who came to Lydney for cures, and consequently a guest house and bath suite were built to serve their needs.

The bath suite lies to the north of the temple. It was fed by a conduit from a water tank in the centre of the hillfort, and contained the normal range of hot, warm and cold rooms. To the south of the baths lay a long, narrow building, divided into compartments which may have been cubicles for patients taking some form of health cure, or lock-up shops where tourists could purchase votive offerings and souvenirs.

The final building in the group, an extensive guest house measuring some 130 feet by 160 feet, is no longer visible, but clearly provided accommodation for visitors to the temple.

Objects excavated from the Iron Age and Roman sites by Dr. and Mrs. R. E. M. Wheeler in 1928-9, are in the private museum in Lydney Park.

Finally mention may be made of a small motte-and-bailey castle on Little Camp Hill 200 yards south-east of the Iron Age and Roman sites. It was probably built during the reign of King Stephen.

31 Nan Tow's Tump, Didmarton   Bronze Age
    Map 156   ST: 803893
    On the E. side of the A46, some ten miles S. of Stroud, covered with trees.

One of the largest round barrows in the Cotswolds, it stands some 9 feet high and is about 100 feet in diameter. Nan Tow was supposed to have been a local witch who was buried upright in the barrow!

32 Notgrove long barrow   Neolithic
    Map 144   SP: 095212
    Beside the B4068, just E. of the railway bridge. M.P.B.W. signpost.

This chambered long barrow, excavated in 1881 and again in 1934-5 is now in a disgracefully ruinous state. It was originally about 160 feet long and 80 feet wide. It contains the remains of a gallery grave with an ante-chamber and two pairs of side chambers, all open to the sky. Excavation in the chambers produced the remains of at least six adult individuals, as well as three children and a new born baby. Many animal bones, including a young calf, were also present.

Behind the west end of the gallery was a circular domed structure 23 feet in diameter, which had been built before the rest of the tomb. It contained a stone burial cist which held the crouched skeleton of a man of 50 or 60 years. On top of the domed structure were the bones of a young woman of 17 to 19 years of age.

A forecourt between horns of double drystone walling at the east end of the gallery grave revealed signs of fires, the bones of animals and the skeletons of two young people. These seem to indicate an elaborate burial ritual. The whole tomb displayed evidence to show that it had been robbed on a number of occasions since Iron Age and Roman times. The finds from the excavations are in Cheltenham Museum.

33 Nottingham Hill hillfort, Gotherington   Iron Age
Map 144   SO:984284
Minor road N.W. from A46 ¼ mile N.E. of Cleeve Hill. A farm road runs through the fort. Muddy in bad weather.

This north facing spur, 915 feet above sea level, juts out from the Cotswold ridge into the vale of Gloucester. Although Oxenton Hill rises in front of it, its greater height allows it to look across to the hillforts on the outlying Bredon Hill 6 and 7 miles away.

The flat top of Nottingham Hill is surrounded by a remarkably unimpressive bank and ditch, which is doubled on the south-east side. These double banks and ditches on the south-east are very strong and are set closely to each other. The inner bank is still 10 feet high, the other 7 feet high above the outer ditch. This is the main feature on the site, and it may be seen to serve the function of a cross-dyke isolating the 120 acre promontory spur on the north-west. Such an area may perhaps be regarded as containing a single agricultural unit. There may have been an entrance at the north corner overlooking Prescott House, or more probably at the south-east corner, now quarried away.

34 Nympsfield long barrow, Frocester   Neolithic
Map 156   SO:794013
On W. side of B4066, marked 'Burial Chambers' on O.S. maps.

This chambered long barrow which lies east to west, is 90 feet long and 60 feet wide. It was excavated in 1862 and re-excavated in 1937 because of its 'deplorable condition'. It has since been left open to the sky to deteriorate even more rapidly. The barrow contained a cross-shaped stone-lined gallery with one pair of side chambers and an end chamber. The mound of the barrow is enclosed by a dry-stone wall which is now covered by barrow rubble. At the horned east end this wall is doubled, and at the narrower west end it is concave. Post holes and ashes of fires were found in this west area. In the horned forecourt of the barrow was another area of burning and a small pit. Elaborate funeral rituals were probably carried out in each area. Between 20 and 30 burials came from the barrow during the two excavations, as well as Neolithic pottery and a leaf-shaped arrow head. The finds from the 1937 excavations are in Stroud Museum.

35 Painswick Beacon (Kimsbury, or Castle Godwin)
Iron Age
Map 143   SO: 869121
Parking on minor road linking A46 with B4073 at N. end of golf course.

This multivallate hillfort is sited on a prominent spur of the Cotswolds overlooking Gloucester. Much of the interior of the site has been badly damaged by quarrying and the laying-out of a golf course. Closely set double ramparts and ditches with a counterscarp bank exist on the west, south and east sides, and enclose a triangular area of about 7 acres. Traces of these ramparts without ditches can be seen along the steep north scarp. The main entrance is near the south-east end, where the inner rampart has long, sharply inturned ends. A second possible entrance could have existed in the north-west corner where an inturning of the surviving rampart meets a deep hollow-way. Due to the quarrying activities no interior features can be identified with certainty, except for a large funnel-shaped hollow 9 feet deep, of unknown date and purpose in the centre of the camp.

36 Pole's Wood South long barrow, Swell   Neolithic
Map 144   SP: 167264
Farm track W. from minor road linking Upper and Lower Swell.

This damaged and irregular chambered long barrow measures 180 feet long, 70 feet wide and 10 feet high. Its higher end seems to have been horned with a forecourt, but there is no record of either an entrance or false entrance. A burial chamber, still visible, near the north side of the narrower west end, was entered by an approach passage, 6 feet long. Excavation in this chamber in 1874 produced the remains of at least 9 individuals, together with animal bones and Neolithic pot sherds, whilst 3 other skeletons lay in the entrance passage.

Three Saxon burials had been placed near the surface of the barrow many centuries later. They included a man with an iron spearhead and knife, and a woman with two saucer brooches and an amber bead.

Other barrows in the vicinity include **Pole's Wood East long barrow** (SP:172265) 500 yards north-east, which had a horned forecourt and an enclosed burial chamber containing 19 skeletons and Neolithic pottery when excavated in 1875-6. The barrow still stands 5 feet high, 120 feet long and 40 feet wide, but the chamber is no longer visible.

The **Lower Swell long barrow** (SP:170258) is 150 feet long, 50 feet wide and 10 feet high. It stands in a spinney surrounded by a ploughed field. The standing stone known as the **Hoar Stone** (SP:170248) may once have been part of another burial chamber. **The Tump,** (SP:166259) ½ mile west of Lower Swell is a round barrow now planted with trees and surrounded by a drystone wall. It is about 60 feet in diameter and 5 feet high. There are many more round barrows in this vicinity.

37 Randwick long barrow   Neolithic
Map 156   SO: 825069
Situated in Standish Wood (National Trust) on the summit of the hill N.W. of Randwick church.

This ruined chambered long barrow is still about 180 feet long, 80 feet wide and 10 feet high. When dug in 1883 the horned entrance led directly to a single burial chamber which contained a mass of human bones, some 'very old British' pottery and three flint flakes. There were also Roman remains which suggested that the barrow might have been robbed at that time. The remains of several crouched skeletons were found outside the south-west end of the barrow. Mr. G. B. Witts, the digger, considered that these were slaves buried with their chief.

38 Rodmarton Windmill Tump   Neolithic
Map 157   ST: 932978
Tree covered, in the middle of a ploughed field, S. of the minor road between Rodmarton and Cherington.

Like the majority of Cotswold long barrows, Windmill

46

Tump lies east to west. It is about 200 feet long and 70 feet wide, and is contained within a modern wall. There is a fine false entrance at the east end. On either side of the barrow are rectangular burial chambers approached by passages and three steps down. The south chamber contained fragments of several skeletons and prehistoric pottery. The north chamber held 10 adult skeletons and 3 children. Both had porthole entrances (see Avening) with their original blocking. At present the chambers are inaccessible.

39 Salmonsbury Camp, Bourton   Iron Age
Map 144   SP: 175208
Between Bourton-on-the-Water and the river Dickler.
An unimpressive lowland camp, square in shape, which encloses some 56 acres, this was originally protected on at least two sides by marshes. The defences consist of an inner loose gravel bank, now only 2½ feet high and 60 feet wide, separated from an outer bank by a V-shaped ditch 34 feet wide and 12 feet deep. A filled-in outer ditch was 19 feet wide and 9 feet deep. There was probably a stone wall on top of the inner rampart, but evidence of ploughing of the site in Roman times, suggests that the wall was thrown into the ditch during that time.

Excavation in 1931 revealed the foundations of a wooden hut 22 feet in diameter, which consisted of a ring of eighteen post-holes and three central holes for supporting a roof. An entrance 8 feet wide faced south.

A hoard of 147 iron currency bars was found on the north-west side of the camp in 1860, which, with the pottery from the site, suggest a date for occupation in the 1st century B.C. Pits of 3rd and 2nd century B.C. date beneath the rampart indicate that the site was inhabited long before fortification took place.

40 Sodbury Camp, Chipping Sodbury   Iron Age
Map 156 (Plate 10)   ST: 760826
Access by farm road from A46 on E. or from Portway Lane from Chipping Sodbury. The site is normally under grass.
This is one of the finest multivallate hillforts on the edge of the Cotswolds escarpment. Rectangular in shape, it encloses about 11 acres. On the north, east and south, are widely spaced double ramparts 100 feet apart. The inner rampart of glacis construction stands 5 feet above the interior of the camp, and 13 feet above the exterior. This bank curves round the north-

west corner and runs halfway along the west side. The silted ditch outside the inner rampart is 26 feet wide and 7 feet deep. The main entrance is midway along the east side, where the rampart ends are slightly overlapped. The core of the rampart, composed of fire-reddened limestone, is clearly visible at this point.

There are indications that the outer rampart is unfinished, since it is irregular in height, although in places reaching 12 feet high. A wide berm separates it from an equally irregular outer ditch which fades out on the north side. This rampart and ditch are broken in two places along the east side. Although the south break, opposite the entrance in the inner rampart is the most logical for access to the camp, there is a possibility that the north break may also have been an entrance gap. The rampart at this point is out-turned, and there appears to have been a guard-chamber on the north side.

41 Soldier's Grave barrow, Nympsfield
Bronze Age
Map 156
SO: 794015
On W. side of B4066, in wood 230 yards N. of Nymps-field long barrow.

This unusual round barrow which is 56 feet in diameter, was found on excavation to contain a rock-cut boat shaped grave, lined with drystone walling. It measured 11 feet long, $4\frac{1}{2}$ feet wide and $3\frac{3}{4}$ feet deep. It contained the scattered remains of at least 28 people, and pieces of Early Bronze Age pottery. This seems to represent a mixture of Neolithic ideas of collective burial and Bronze Age round barrow burial, and the grave is probably of transitional date. The burial chamber is not visible.

42 Tingle Stone long barrow, Avening
Neolithic
Map 156
ST: 882990
W. of the minor road from Avening Church to Hampton Fields, and at S.E. corner of Gatcombe Park.

This barrow gets its name from the oolite standing stone 6 feet high at its north end. Unusual in that the barrow, which is 70 feet long, lies north to south, it is planted with beech trees and no chambers have been found. There is a local folk tradition that the Tingle Stone runs round the field when it hears the clock strike twelve!

43 Uleybury hillfort, Uley
Iron Age
Map 156
ST: 785990
Access from B4066 at West Hill, or by footpaths from Uley or Crawley.

One of the finest promontory hillforts in the Cotswolds. At all points except the north corner the ground falls steeply 300 feet to the valley below. A rampart and a silted ditch enclose some 32 acres. Lower down the hillside is a slighter ditch about 7 feet wide with a low rampart on the outer side. The main entrance at the north corner is defended by a mound and three ditches cutting across the narrow ridge which connects the promontory with the main Cotswold massif. Other apparently original entrances occur at the south and east corners where hollow-ways approach up the hillside. The rampart on either side of the south entrance terminates in a conspicuous mound. The site has not been excavated, but an uninscribed Dobunic gold stater is amongst finds from the fort now in Gloucester City Museum. The interior of the camp is normally arable.

44 Windrush Camp, Windrush
Iron Age
Map 144   SP: 181123
S. of A40 between Northleach and Burford. Approached by farm road.

A roughly circular plateau fort enclosing about 6½ acres, sited on level ground above the Windrush valley. Of the single bank and ditch, only the bank is now visible, the ditch having silted up and long been ploughed over. The entrance was probably on the west side.

45 Woodchester Roman villa
Roman
Map 156   ST: 840030
On N. of village and S. of old churchyard. Mosaic floors uncovered at irregular intervals for exhibition.

This great courtyard villa with at least sixty-four rooms was excavated by Samuel Lysons late in the 18th century. The rooms were ranged round two courtyards and contain some of the finest mosaics in Britain including one of the early 4th century showing Orpheus, and probably one containing a fountain at its centre. Much more of this house, including the baths, awaits discovery.

OXFORDSHIRE

1 Alchester Roman town
Roman
Map 145/6   SP: 573202
Two miles S.W. of Bicester, on minor (Roman) road branching S. of A421.

This small town is completely ploughed. Only the slightly raised earthwork around it stands above the neighbouring fields to a height of 3 or 4 feet. The raised causeway of a road can be seen entering the town at the centre of the north side.

2 Chastleton Burrow Camp   Iron Age
Map 144 (Plate 7)   SP: 259283
Off the A436, beside the road signposted to Chastleton House. Gated footpath from road N.W. of camp.

This circular fort encloses 3½ acres. It is unusual in that its defences are faced with large blocks of stone, and probably have a rubble core, and yet there is no sign of a ditch from which the material was quarried. Excavation showed that the wall was 20 feet wide at the base, and still stands 12 feet high in places today. There was no sign of any permanent occupation. There were two entrances, one at the east, the other north-west. The camp may have served as a cattle enclosure: modern cattle are rapidly destroying it.

3 Dyke Hills, Dorchester-on-Thames   Iron Age/Roman
Map 158 (Plate 11)   SU: 574937
A footpath leads from the S. end of Dorchester, N. of the river bridge.

Dyke Hills is the name given to the earthwork isolating a low-lying promontory fort situated between an angle of the Thames and the Thame. Some 114 acres are enclosed by two large banks and ditches running east to west across the north end of the peninsula. The other sides are protected by the two rivers. There are a number of gaps in the ramparts, but all seem to be modern, and the position of an original entrance is unknown, but it may well have been on the east side, where it could be aligned with a road leaving the Roman town of Dorchester. Aerial photographs show that the enclosed area contains many pits, circles and rectangular enclosures of a settlement site. It is possible that the fort represented a local Iron Age town, which was later replaced by the small Roman township of Dorchester-on-Thames.

Roman Dorchester was a rectangular walled town of about 13½ acres, and lay under the south-west quadrant of the modern town, west of Dorchester Abbey. Although no buildings remain today, the line of the defences, a denuded bank and wide ditch-hollow can still be seen round three-quarters of the circuit, especially to the east of Watling Lane, in the area occupied by allotments (SU: 578941). Excavations in the allotments in 1962 revealed a late Roman building and an early Saxon hut, together with traces of later Saxon buildings.

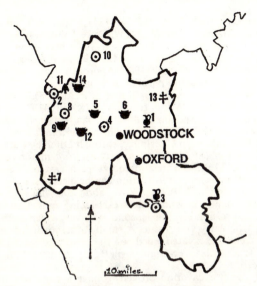

Archaeological sites in Oxfordshire

The earth rampart was erected round the town in the 2nd century A.D., and subsequently between A.D. 270 and 290 a stone wall was built in front of this rampart. The town continued in use into the 5th century, when Roman troops of some kind were garrisoned in the town.

Nothing remains of **The Big Rings** and other Neolithic henge monuments, excavated at Dorchester between 1946-50, which were all discovered by aerial photography, and have now been totally destroyed by gravel quarrying (SU : 573954).

4 Grim's Ditch, North Oxfordshire   Iron Age
Map 145   Various

At least five lengths of Grim's Ditch occur in the triangle between Charlbury, Kiddington and Woodstock. These ditch sections all seem to have been constructed across stretches of open country, in between areas of woodland. They were dug during the 1st century A.D. by Belgic Iron Age people moving west from Hertfordshire. They seem to have isolated an area between the rivers Evenlode on the west and Glynne on the east, with the dykes facing north. The best sections to view are at :

51

1 *Blenheim Great Park* (SP:427183). Approach on foot through Ditchley Gate of B4437. Dyke ½ mile south crosses drive. A gap in the dyke seems to have been used by the Romans as a crossing place for the Akerman Street.

2 *Glympton Farm* (SP:423197). Approach along cart-track of A34. Runs roughly parallel to main road.

3 *Out Wood and Berrings Wood* (SP:413208). Footpath through Berrings Wood from A34 (at SP:419209). Both butt-ends of this section of the dyke can be clearly seen.

4 *Home Farm* (SP:402215). Visible beside minor road from Over Kiddington to Charlbury, through Ditchley Park.

5 *Model Farm* (SP:383209). Approach from minor road (4 above) to Model Farm and follow path east beside dyke. The east butt-end of this section can be clearly seen.

Callow Hill (SP:383209). Here two additional lines of ditch can be seen faintly crossing a low east facing spur. Both cross the B4437. Presumably this ground was very open and considered particularly vulnerable. A small Romano-British settlement has been excavated north of the road and west of the ditches. Traces of a rectangular platform for a building can still be seen.

The dyke on excavation proved to have a bank which was 20 feet broad and about 6 feet high, with a V-shaped ditch of similar width and 6 feet deep in front of it.

5 Hoar Stone long barrow, Enstone   Neolithic
Map 145   SP:378236

In a small walled enclosure at the N. end of Enstone plantation, at junction of B4022 with Enstone-Ditchley road.

This is the ruined remnant of a chambered long barrow. Three rough stones, the largest 9 feet high, form a roofless U-shaped chamber, with an opening facing east. Three fallen stones lie in front of the chamber and must once have formed part of it. The mound of the long barrow, still standing 3 feet high in 1824, has now completely disappeared, and a reservoir has been constructed immediately behind the monument to the west.

6 Hoar Stone long barrow, Steeple Barton   Neolithic
Map 145   SP:458241

In a wood midway along the bridle road from Barton Abbey to the Rousham Gap-Wootton road.

A long barrow, 50 feet in length, with a pile of broken

sandstones at its east end, is probably the remains of a chambered long barrow described in the last century.

7 Langford, St. Matthew's church
Anglo Saxon

Map 157 (Plate 15)
SP: 248025

In the S.W. corner of Oxfordshire.

St. Matthew's has an Anglo Saxon tower and sundial and two fascinating carvings, now displayed on the porch exterior. Both carvings show the Crucifixion. In one Christ (headless) is shown in priest's attire: this has been dated to the early part of the 11th century. The other, incorrectly mounted on the wall, shows Christ on the cross with the Virgin and St. John on either side. This carving is probably a little later than the other, perhaps mid-11th century.

8 Lyneham Camp hillfort
Iron Age

Map 145
SP: 299214

Beside the A361. Gate on to main road in trees just N. of minor road junction.

A roughly circular camp enclosing 4½ acres. It is surrounded by a single well-marked bank and ditch, which have been destroyed by a quarry and the A361 road on the south-east. The bank still stands 6 feet high in places and is faced with drystone walling. The ditch, which can be clearly seen in the wood to the west, is U-shaped and has been proved by excavation to be 18 feet wide and 7 feet deep. There is a gap in the rampart facing north which may have been an original entrance. Like Chastleton Camp, 6 miles north-west, Lyneham may have been used as a cattle enclosure.

9 Lyneham long barrow
Neolithic

Map 145
SP: 297211

On W. side of A361, ¼ mile S. of Lyneham Camp.

A single upright stone 6 feet high and 5 feet broad stands at the north-east end of this long barrow, and may once have formed part of a false entrance. The mound, which is now 160 feet long, has been considerably reduced by ploughing, as can be seen from the scatter of stone in the field around. The remains of two apparently unconnected burial chambers were found in excavations in 1894, and skulls and animal and human bones were found scattered throughout the mound. Two Saxon graves were also uncovered at that time. Numerous holes in the top suggest various other diggings. The site is overgrown with bushes, and traces of an old field wall run across the east end of the barrow.

10 Madmarston hillfort
Iron Age

Map 145   SP:386389

Bridle road N.W. of Tadmarton from Lower Lea Farm towards Farmington Farm.

This fort of 5¼ acres is rectangular in shape and is surrounded by two banks with a ditch between them, and an additional bank and ditch on the south and west sides. All the earthworks have suffered badly from ploughing. An entrance lay in the centre of the south side. Excavation has shown that the site was first occupied in the Southern Second B phase of the Iron Age, when coarse hand-made pottery and metalwork was produced, and a cattle-raising economy was practised. After a period of desertion the site was re-occupied late in Romano-British times (4th century A.D.) when it was again a centre of agricultural activity.

There was also a Romano-British settlement, some 300 yards south-east of the fort, close to the Swalcliffe Lea Farm.

11 Rollright Stones
Bronze Age

Map 145 (Plates 4, 5)   SP:296308

Beside the ridge road which follows the county boundary from Great Rollright W. to the A436, ½ mile N. of Little Rollright church. Ministry of Public Building and Works; open at any time.

The Rollright Stones, together with the Whispering Knights chambered barrow ¼ mile east, form the most celebrated group of prehistoric antiquities in Oxfordshire. They have long attracted attention and are the subject of a considerable amount of folklore.

The King's Men. This consists of a circle of about 70 stones, with a diameter of 100-110 feet. No attempt has been made to shape the stones which present a gnarled and weathered appearance, and are 'corroded like worm-eaten wood by the harsh jaws of time'. There is a legend that the stones are countless. The site is unexcavated.

The King Stone. Situated a few yards east of the circle on the north (Warwickshire) side of the road. This standing stone is 8 feet high and 5 feet wide, and like the King's Men, is very weathered. It has been considered to be part of the chamber of a long barrow which is said to have lain to the north but this seems unlikely. There is certainly a long ridge, called by Stukeley 'The Archdruid's Barrow', but excavation has shown it to be natural. Isolated standing stones are not an uncommon feature in association with stone circles.

The Whispering Knights (SP:299308). Although ¼ mile east of the King's Men (a track leads to them beside a hedgerow),

54

these stones are part of the Rollright tradition. They probably formed the chamber of a long barrow. Four stones still stand upright forming a chamber about 6 feet square, whilst a fifth stone, probably the cover-stone, leans at an angle. The stones vary in height between 5 and 8 feet. Although Stukeley (1746) claimed that the stones stood on a round barrow, only the slightest trace of any mound is visible today and its shape is quite uncertain.

Of all the Rollright legends, the most famous tells how a king was riding across Oxfordshire, accompanied by his knights and men, when he was challenged by a witch, who said:

> Seven long strides thou shalt take,
> And if Long Compton thou can see,
> King of England thou shalt be.

Whilst the king's knights whispered together about what they heard, and the men stood by in a circle, the king strode forward seven paces; but instead of seeing Long Compton in the valley below, the long mound 'The Archdruid's Barrow' blocked the way. Then with a cackle the witch exclaimed:

> As Long Compton thou canst not see,
> King of England thou shalt not be,
> Rise up stick, and stand still stone,
> For King of England thou shalt be none.
> Thou and thy men hoar stones shall be,
> And I myself an elder tree.

12 Slatepits Copse long barrow, Wychwood — Neolithic
Map 145   SP:329165

In a clearing in Wychwood Forest, ¼ mile E. of the Leafield-Charlbury road.

This chambered long barrow is 100 feet long, 45 feet wide and 6 feet high. It lies east to west with a much-ruined burial chamber composed of 3 upright stones, at the east end. It is recorded that three skulls were found in the chamber in the middle of the last century.

13 Stuttle's Bank, Stratton Audley — Danish?
Map 145/6   SP:625283

On W. side of minor road from Stratton Audley to Chetwode, in new copse opposite Oldfields Copse, on N. side of track through trees.

This earthwork consists of a bank enclosing an amphitheatre-like depression, 93 feet in diameter. There is an apparent entrance on the north side. There is higher ground above the site, which slopes down towards a small stream ½ mile to the north. The earthwork seems to belong to a series of ring-works probably attributable to the Danes.

14 Whispering Knights long barrow

Neolithic

Map 145 (Plate 4)

SP: 299308

Fully described under *Rollright Stones*, page 54.

Printed by Maund & Irvine Ltd., Tring, Herts.